*A Young Person's Book
of
Catholic Signs and Symbols*

A YOUNG PERSON'S BOOK OF CATHOLIC SIGNS AND SYMBOLS

Francis Tiso

NAZARETH BOOKS™
Doubleday & Company, Inc.
Garden City, New York
1982

Nazareth Books is a trademark of
The Catholic Heritage Press, Inc.

Project Directors for Nazareth Books

John J. Kirvan

Roger J. Radley

First Edition

CONTENTS

INTRODUCTION

We are blessed with eyes. Our eyes look out on the world and give us information and excitement that it would be very difficult to receive in any other way. Can you imagine having no eyes? With your eyes closed, you could use your hands to feel a carved piece of wood; you could use your fingers to probe the designs in the handle of a fork; you could guess at the height of a friend by placing your hand on his or her head while you were both standing straight up. But without your eyes you would never know what a "red" is, or a "green"; you would have no idea what a sparkle of sunlight on rippling waves might be; you would never know if someone's glance was cold and angry or deep, warm and kind. A deer at the forest edge would be invisible to you, and you would never know the doe's excitement as she lifts the tuft of her white tail just before she leaps into the wood.

Yet we know that God is not visible to our eyes. True, we may sometimes imagine God in our minds. No two people will have exactly the same picture of God in their minds. Even from day to day, our ideas and images of God may change. This is because we are always experiencing life in new ways. Each day, we grow older, we learn more, we forget some things and we remember other things, we invent stories and meet new friends. As our life changes, we learn to imagine God at work in new ways in our lives. We have much to learn from God, and he is a patient friend who has something new for us every day. Are we ready every day for what God has in store for us? If we have become good watchers, good listeners and good responders, we may be able to catch up with God; God and his story run on ahead of us, and then surprise us by coming up on us from behind! There are ways by which we can train ourselves to watch for the signs of God's presence. The best way is to spend a little time each day in quiet, speaking to God, praying to God, imagining God, and wondering what he is going to show us today. This is the "inner" training that enables us to see with our "inner eyes," the "eyes of our heart."

Then there is the world we see with our outer eyes, the organs of sight. Is there any connection between what we see in our hearts with our imagination and feelings and what we see with our body's eyes? Has God left us signs that we can see, by which we can know that he and his story have passed by a particular person or place?

When we follow a deer through the forest, we can see his tracks on the snow or soft clay soil. Nothing but a deer could have left that print! The deer sign assures us that a deer has passed by not long ago. Did you ever wonder if the deer, too, can read signs? The signs of people: footprints of hiking boots, cans and bottles, campfires, wood cut for walking sticks and firewood.

There is an old story that the deer watch for hunters in their forests. The deer chase the hunters in and out of swamps, rocky ground, and woodlands. At the edge of a meadow, one deer "catches" a hunter. The hunter has to shoot the deer, drain his blood, and make him ready to take home for food. The hunter and his family eat the deer and the deer comes back to life inside the people he has "caught." The deer, it turns out, are very wise in their dealings with people.

In dealing with the signs of our faith, the signs that God leaves in the world by which we can find him, we are also on a kind of hunt in a forest thick with trees. There are a few paths cut through the forest by wise woodsmen and by the wise women who go there searching for herbs to heal the sick. You, too, can go on a hike through these woods, searching for the signs that tell us where God has passed by. Perhaps you will find that he has been nearby recently; in some places, his presence first arrived long ago. But even in the very oldest places, you can sense his power, the power of his story. You can feel God reaching out to you in these holy places, the signs and symbols of our faith. These signs of God's presence, his love and caring for us, make up a great story, a story you will pass on to your children and grandchildren as it was passed on to me. Just as the deer comes to life again in the people who ate him, so also does the wisdom of God live on in those who watch and listen and take his signs and symbols to heart.

THE ONE GOD

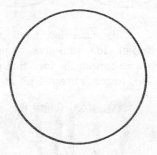

The One. Circle. The circle is the greatest and simplest symbol of God, who is one, and simple, and full of love. In the Bible we read: "Hear, O Israel! The Lord, your God, is One, one God Alone. And you shall love the Lord, your God, with your whole heart and your whole mind, and your whole strength; and you shall love your neighbor as yourself."

The Trinity. God is made known to us as One in love, but he has also shown us that His Oneness is a love that is shared by three Divine Persons: the Father, the Son, and the Holy Spirit. The Son is Jesus Christ, who is a true human being,

our brother, and at the same time he is perfectly One with God. He is the Son of God, who gives us the gift of the Holy Spirit so that we can share in the love that unites Jesus Christ to the Father, God, who has created all of us and our world.

YAHWEH. This is the Name of God, revealed by God to Moses in ancient times, just before he led the Israelites out of their slavery in the land of oppression. It means: I AM WHO I AM. The name Jesus in Hebrew is Yeshua, a name that means YAHWEH-saves-us. In Jesus, we meet God, whose holy name is I AM WITH YOU ALWAYS.

Father. When Jesus taught his disciples to pray, he told them to say, "Our Father, who art in heaven. . . ." Jesus taught us that God is very near to us, he is a father who gives us life, who loves us and who cares for us every day of our lives, be-

cause we can ask him confidently to "give us this day our daily bread." Since God is our Father, every human person is a brother or sister, and Jesus, too, is our brother, a brother who shows us the kind of love that comes straight from God.

Burning Bush. Fire. Glory. When the Lord God revealed to Moses that his Holy Name is Yahweh, I AM WHO I AM, he appeared as fire in a bush in the desert. If you have ever been in a desert, you know that you can see a long distance in the flatlands, and every scraggly tree or bush stands out. The desert is empty, but when something unusual comes along, it is all the more noticeable. So when Moses saw a burning bush, he could not help but go over for a look. And in those miraculous flames, he saw the presence of God. The brightness of the light of God and the heat of God is called his "glory." The great prophet Moses was guided and strengthened by the glory of God to carry out the hard task of leading his people to freedom.

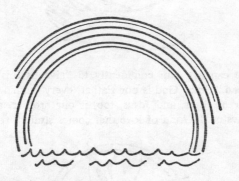

The Rainbow of the Covenant. Long ago, a man named Noah and his family escaped drowning in a large wooden ship called the Ark. On board the Ark were all kinds of animals and the seeds of plants, so that Noah could restore the land as it was before the great Flood. After many days and nights, the waters grew shallower and shallower. The tips of mountains appeared. Then trees, and finally the ground could be seen again. Mud was everywhere. In the sky, a great rainbow appeared as a sign. God assured Noah that never again would the world have to fear a great Flood, and every time we see a rainbow we are to be reminded of our friendship with God. This friendship is called a "covenant," and God will never turn his back on those people he has chosen as his partners and friends. Our job is to make this a world of peace and love and never to turn away from the God who cares for us.

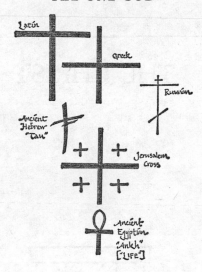

The Tau. The Seal of the Living God. The Cross.

THE CHRIST

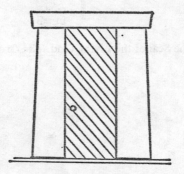

The Door. The Door is a very powerful symbol. We can close off a space with a door, or we can open a pathway into the house by opening the door. An open door is a sign of welcome; a closed door keeps us *out*. Jesus says that he himself is the Door and that by this Door we can enter the fullness of life that the Father has prepared for us. We pass to a new life through Jesus and leave behind all our past mistakes and failures. Jesus is the open Door, who welcomes us into the Kingdom of his Father, where love is the only law (Jn 10:1–2, 7–9; Ps 24:7–9; 118:19–20).

The True Vine. A symbol of Jesus and the union of believers with him. We are dependent on Jesus for the deeper life the Father wants to share with us.

Each year, a grapevine produces many new shoots. Left untended, the vine would soon produce huge numbers of leaves and branches but less and less fruit. In order to make the vine produce grapes, it must be pruned back every year. Different kinds of grapes can be grafted onto the one "stock," or main vine. Jesus compared our union with him to the union of branches with the stock. We are united to Jesus through the Church and the sacraments. Since grapes are used to make the wine for Mass, a grapevine always reminds us of the sacraments and the special closeness we experience with Jesus in the sacraments, especially the Eucharist. Jesus fills us with divine life, just as the stock of the vine sends nourishment to the branches. Jesus underwent suffering so that his life would be more fruitful for others. So, too, the vine is cut and pruned to produce more grapes. Every Christian, too, must be "pruned" by discipline and suffering in union with the sufferings of Jesus. The Christian suffers joyfully, knowing that from suffering can come great good (Jn 15:2).

The Bronze Serpent. A symbol of Christ on the cross as our Healer and the Giver of everlasting life.

The serpent itself is a symbol of sin and rebellion, because it was the serpent who tempted Eve in the Garden of Eden. But when the Israelites were journeying in the desert in the days of Moses, many of them were bitten by snakes. God told Moses (Nb 21:8–9) to make a magic serpent of bronze and set it up on a pole so that anyone who had been bitten by a snake could look at the bronze serpent and be cured. Jesus says: ". . . the Son of Man must be lifted up as Moses lifted up the serpent in the desert, so that everyone who believes may have eternal life in him" (Jn 3:13–15). When we look at Jesus on the cross, we are reminded that he has healed us from the snakebites of our sins and that he offers us a new way to live.

Rock, Cornerstone. The rock symbolizes Christ as the center of our lives and the source of refreshment. When the Israelites were following Moses in the desert, they received water from a rock that Moses struck with his staff. So, too, from Jesus we receive "living waters": the teachings and graces of the Christian life. Jesus is the Cornerstone of our faith, the Keystone of the main arch of our spiritual building, the Church. He is that strong stone that completes the great rainbow arch of creation according to the plans of God our Father. Remember that Jesus said: "The stone which the builders rejected has become the cornerstone" (Ps 118:22–23; Lk 20:17–18). Rejection by people's opinions carries no weight in the plan of God. In Christ's building there is room for everyone, every shape and kind of stone—that is, every kind of person.

The Good Shepherd. Jesus said: "I am the Good Shepherd; I know my own and my own know me; as the Father knows me, and I know the Father. And I lay down my life for the sheep" (Jn 10:14–15).

The Good Shepherd knows each one of the sheep in his flock. He knows their names and they respond to his voice. He keeps the flock safe and united; the sheep know that he cares for them. We, too, must listen to recognize the voice of Jesus, our Shepherd, calling us to the ways of his gospel. This listening is learned in prayer.

The Grain of Wheat. The grain is planted in the earth and "dies" in order to germinate and produce new life. It is a symbol of God's power to make new life; in the dying of Jesus, and in his rising from the dead, we see the same pattern. Jesus' self-giving love leads him to death on a cross; the power of God's love raises him to new life, a life we can all share by following Jesus daily by living generously and motivated by love, by being courageous enough to die for what is right, by being unselfish and understanding in our attitude toward others. We have a great hope as we live the Christian life for blessings on all in the Kingdom of God.

Labarum. The standard on which Roman soldiers hung the banner of their legion. The Emperor Constantine changed his labarum when he became a Christian; he put the name "Christ" on his banner. The labarum has come to be a symbol of the resurrection of Christ (cf. p. 55).

> "The royal banners forward go,
> The Cross shines forth in mystic glow
> Where He, as Man, who gave man breath,
> Now bows beneath the yoke of death."

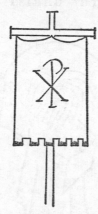

This ancient hymn celebrates the death of Jesus on the cross as the victory of the Kingdom of heaven. God's reign begins to spread across the earth as the gospel of Jesus is proclaimed. Although it appeared that Jesus had been defeated by death, in fact He has risen from the dead and has made the instrument of death, the cross, a sign of the victory of life. The banner of Christ the King is the cross, now a sign of *God's* power to renew our lives (cf. p. 22).

Son of Man. The image of a great human figure glowing with light and power in the sky was one of Daniel's visions in the Hebrew Scriptures. This vision of the Son of Man came to be a symbol of many things: the glorified people of Israel standing as a sign, before all nations, of the love of God; the Messiah, who would save Israel and renew the relationship between God and his people, and finally, the mysterious figure who would come to proclaim the end of history and the beginning of the reign of God across the whole of creation. Jesus referred to himself as the Son of Man, who would fulfill

all the prophecies himself in his suffering, death, and Resurrection. Catholic tradition tells us that the Son of Man refers to Jesus in his human nature.

Son of David. (Ps 132:11–12; 2 S 7:12–16; Mt 21:9) The Lord promised David, the king of all the tribes of Israel, that not only would his son Solomon become king after him, but also that his royal family would endure forever. But after a few centuries, David's royal descendants had been carried off into Babylon as subjects, and others had been killed. Had God been untrue to his word? Was the promise to David empty (see Ps 44)? Or had we misunderstood the ways of God? When Jesus was born, he was recognized as king by the Magi (Mt 2:2) and as a descendant of David (Mt 1:1). Thus, Christians came to see that the promise made to David was to be fulfilled in Jesus, his descendant, who would be a king forever, in a new way. Jesus is a king who continually gives himself in service to his people: to all of us who seek his friendship and all who are in need. Thus, the royal line of David continues forever in the Kingdom of love and peace.

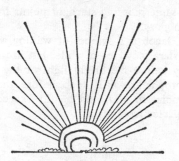

Rising Sun. (Lk 1:78) The early Christians faced east, toward the rising sun, when they prayed every morning. This was a way of remembering the Resurrection of Jesus from the dead. His death was like nightfall, and his rising like a glowing sunrise renewing the life of all the sleeping earth. Jesus is a new light in the world, brighter than all other lights. The sun's bright light reminds us of the spiritual light of Jesus Christ.

Someday, rise early and watch the sun rise. Do you feel the power of that new light coming across the earth? What else do you feel at that time?

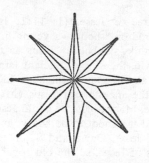

Star of Jacob. (Nb 24:17; Mt 2:2; Rv 22:16) Jesus' birth was announced by a star that the wise men followed to Bethlehem. This is the "morning star," the brightest star just before sunrise, which anticipates the resurrection light of sunrise. And this same morning starlight points toward the coming of Christ in glory.

The Star of Jacob is a symbol of waiting and expectation. The morning stars glow for a while, but are soon overcome and fade away before the bright light of the rising sun. So, too, do the prophetic words fade before the brightness of Christ. They point to him; and he far exceeds anything we might have expected from them.

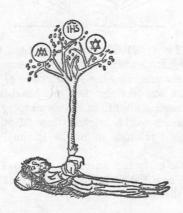

Rod of Jesse. Tree of Jesse. (Is 11:1; Jr 23:5; Zc 6:12; Rv 22:16) This rod or "shoot"—a young branch growing out of an old tree trunk—symbolizes Jesus as the descendant of the family of David, the king of ancient Israel. David's father was named Jesse and lived in Bethlehem. In the Tree of Jesse, we see many of the ancestors of Jesus (Mt 1) portrayed. At the top of the tree, Mary holds the Child Jesus. Medieval symbolism understood the shoot to be Mary, and its flower Jesus.

The lineage of Jesse, David and Solomon no longer ruled Israel in the days of Jesus, so the old royal tree *looked* dead. But, in Jesus, the "Son of David," a new and eternal life entered our world.

Key of David. (Is 22:22; Mt 16:19; Rv 3:7) The key of David is his royal power and authority. The king alone can open his towns and cities, their storerooms and treasures,

their forts and prisons. So, too, Jesus, as the true heir of David, has the key of David, full authority to forgive sin and to save the whole human race. He has the key to free all of us and to enter into our hearts. Jesus passed on this authority to the apostles (led by Peter). The ministry of "opening and closing," the power to use the keys, has been handed down to the successors of Peter, the popes.

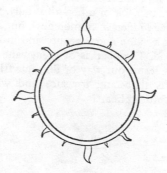

Sun of Justice. (Ml 4:1–2; Mt 17:1–2; Rv 1:16) Christ is the "Sun of God's justice," who brings a new era of truth, fairness, and peace to the world. Our life as Christians is turned toward Christ, just as plants turn toward the sunlight.

Since Jesus rose from the dead on a Sunday, we find the sun's daily rising a symbol of Jesus' power to conquer death every day.

Our work on earth is to create a world where peace and justice are as common as sunlight and air.

The Precious Pearl. (Mt 7:6; 13:45–46; Rv 21:21) An oyster has a very rutty, irregular shell, and soft gray flesh inside. How can it make so beautiful and perfect a gem as a pearl? We know that a bit of sand or a chip of shell gets caught in the oyster, and to keep itself from injury, the oyster surrounds the grit with a smooth, shiny layer. Over many years, the layers grow and grow to produce a fine pearl. Found in the depths of the ocean, pearls are used in fine jewelry and in royal crowns. From the humble oyster, the pearl comes to decorate the ears or neck of a beautiful lady. So, too, the wisdom of Christ lies hidden in humbleness, but once it is found, it gives our lives a value and a beauty and meaning that come directly from God. The pearl is of great value, yet how much more valuable is Jesus, our way of life, our friend, whose love is more precious than any treasure and which cannot be stolen from the faithful heart!

Alpha and Omega. (Is 44:6; Rv 1:8, 17; 22:13) Are you fascinated by the letters of the alphabet? Did you ever try to make up new letters or change the shapes of the letters that we use every day? The ancient Jews and Greeks also loved to think about their wonderful alphabets and to play with the letters. Alpha is the first letter of the Greek alphabet (beta is the second, and that is where the word alpha-bet comes from). Omega is the last letter. "From A to Z," we would say. That means *everything*. So when Jesus says, "I am Alpha and Omega," he means he is everything to us, if we let him fill our lives from beginning to end. We should pray often that Jesus will be with us as we start anything and as we finish anything. He will be with us to help us, and he will share our joy when the job is done. We, too, will share his joy with the Father when all that has been begun on earth will find its end and purpose in heaven.

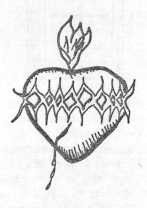

Sacred Heart of Jesus. The heart is the powerful pump that sends our blood coursing through our veins. It is the symbol of our emotions, of our center, of the most important part of our lives. When the heart stops, we quickly die. As long as our hearts are strong, we stay healthy.

The Heart of Jesus is a symbol of his love for us, a center of life and joy for us. Jesus is truly human; he knows how we feel; he can say to any of us, "I have been there, and I am with you now." In fact, he has promised to do just that.

If you place your hand on your heart, you can feel it beating. You can use your imagination to place your hand on the heart of Jesus, to feel it beating in harmony with your own heart. Did you ever use your heart to *listen?* Close your eyes sometime and listen quietly. If you are quiet enough, you might hear your own heartbeat. If you imagine the closeness of Jesus to us, especially after Communion, in that time of deep quiet, you may discover what it is to listen with your heart. You may also find that you are eager to speak and act from your heart, with a new joy and excitement, a joy that comes from Jesus, who is always with us.

Book. Long ago, there were no books. Human beings used other means for exchanging ideas. People sang long songs about their adventures, or danced the stories of the animals and the gods. Then came writing to exchange messages and to record trades and business, to keep lists of people and events and the names of kings, and to let people know who owned what. But could God speak to people through a book? This seemed odd back then—as odd as someone saying today that you can watch God on television. Little by little, people dared to write down even the stories of their gods. In India, the adventures of Krishna and his friend Arjuna in the great wars; in Greece, they wrote down the tales of the battles and romances of gods and heroes; in Egypt, they wrote of Isis and Ra and Osiris. The people of Israel, too, wrote down the words of Yahweh on long scrolls. They wrote down what had happened to them on their long pilgrimage out of Egypt, and the long struggle to be faithful to Yahweh in the Promised Land, and of the many failures that the prophets warned them about. They wrote about what the Lord Yahweh was doing for them *in history* and not so much in legend and saga. These scrolls of laws, history and prophecy came to be held sacred. They are, even today, our holy books, in which the words of God can be read and reread. Since God was willing to speak to humans, a new kind of relationship was possible.

The Word. This new relationship between God and humans came to its highest point in Jesus, whom we call the Word of God. Jesus is not a word that can be written down. He is really a Person that humans can meet. And when people meet Jesus, they are changed, their lives have a new meaning. They feel they have met God in person. Each one of us is a word spoken by God. When each of us hears Jesus, God's first Word, we come to life in a new way. This Person, Jesus, is One with God. God gives us himself perfectly in Jesus. The Bible is our best way to come to know Jesus. Have you read the Gospels? There you can meet the Word, Jesus, in words and stories. Have you shown love and kindness to others? There you can meet the Word, Jesus, in persons.

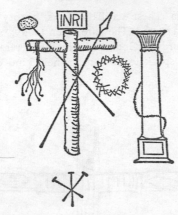

The Crucified Saviour. Christians have meditated for a long time on the sufferings Jesus experienced for our sake. These are represented by the symbols of his passion. In the Gospels, we read of how the soldiers arrested Jesus and brought him to trial. They mocked him, spit in his face, and tied him to a *stone pillar* and whipped him with a leather *whip* that had bits of metal on the ends of the leather strips. They made a *crown* for his head out of *thorns* and forced the thorns into his scalp. Weak and bleeding, he was led before a crowd that demanded his death. They asked that a robber and murderer named Barabbas be set free, but they told Pontius Pilate to have Jesus crucified. So Jesus had the *crossbeam* tied to his shoulders and was led to a little hill outside the city of Jerusalem, where the soldiers nailed his wrists and feet, with *three spikes*, to the wood of the cross. They lifted up the cross and let him hang, bleeding, for three hours. While he was hanging, people came by and made fun of his sufferings, saying that if God were a true friend of his, he would help Jesus come down from the cross. A soldier offered Jesus some sour wine on a *sponge*. He lifted the sponge to Jesus' parched lips on a long stick of reed. Shortly after this, Jesus died.

To be absolutely certain that the condemned men were dead, the Romans would break their legs, causing strangulation. According to the Gospel of John (Jn 19:33–34), the soldiers did not break Jesus' legs. Instead, one of the soldiers plunged a *spear* into the side of Jesus. This opening of his side (and the mysterious flow of blood and water that occurred) has a symbolic meaning for Christians. The pierced body of Christ is looked upon as the new Temple, open wide to all people, where God's abundant love is offered in the form of the sacraments. After the piercing, Jesus' body was taken down from the cross and placed in a new tomb, cut out of rock, nearby. We know that Jesus rose from that tomb "on the third day," but what happened to the cross, the spikes, the reed, the crown of thorns, the whip, and the pillar? And what about the *board* with the saying "Jesus of Nazareth, the King of the Jews," which Pilate had nailed over Jesus' head on the cross? According to legend, all these were lost for many years. Then, around A.D. 320, the mother of the Roman Emperor Constantine, the first Emperor to become a Christian, went on a pilgrimage to Jerusalem to look for the cross. Her name was Helena. She eventually did find the cross, the nails and the board with the title of Jesus on it, and these relics have been revered to this day. Other pilgrims claimed to have found the other relics of the passion of Jesus, bringing them to adorn the churches of Europe in the Middle Ages. You may have heard of the Holy Shroud of Turin, which is believed to be the cloth that the body of Jesus was buried in. Artists have often shown the symbols of the Passion carried by angels in paintings of the Second Coming of Christ, in glory. They intend to remind us that the sufferings of Jesus and indeed all human suffering will be fully revealed at the end of time, when God himself will set all wrongs right and wipe every tear from our eyes.

The Monogram of the Holy Name of Jesus. The letters IHS come from the Greek alphabet and are the first three letters of the name Jesus (Iesous) in Greek. The name Jesus means YAHWEH-is-our-Saviour. It is a "holy name," by which the

human race is saved, healed and brought fully into the orbit of God's love. Just to say the name Jesus can be comforting and strengthening, as many people have found in sickness or distress. Bernardino of Siena was a very great preacher in the 1400s who encouraged his congregations (which filled the town squares all over Italy) to say the Holy Name of Jesus with great love and faith.

Chi-Rho. The monogram that the Emperor Constantine put on his labarum when he became a Christian had the letters Chi and Rho on it. They are the first two letters in the Greek word for Christ. Constantine wanted his soldiers and people to know that his victories belonged not to himself but to a higher Lord, Jesus Christ. This monogram is one of the most familiar Christian symbols of the victory of Christ over death (cf. p. 11).

The Four Living Creatures (the Four Evangelists). This symbolism is taken from Ezekiel 1:4–10 and Revelation 4:2–8. The Four Living Creatures, associated with the Four Evangelists, Matthew, Mark, Luke, and John, are one of the most popular symbols in Christian art. The Four Living Creatures form a perfect square around Christ returning to earth at the end of time in glory to bring all things to completion. Matthew is the figure of a Man, because he begins his Gospel by giving the human ancestors of Christ, both saints and sinners. Mark is the Lion, because he begins his Gospel like a lion in the desert, proclaiming, "Make straight the way of the Lord." This became the symbol of the city of Venice, because the Venetians were devoted to St. Mark. Luke is symbolized by the Ox, which may stand for the animals used in sacrifice at the Temple in Jerusalem, or else it may stand for the ox that warmed Jesus in the manger at his birth in Bethlehem. John is the Eagle, because of his lofty theology of Jesus Christ, the Word of God made flesh, who dwells among us.

The Magi. These astrologers from the East (Mt 2) recognized Christ as King and Messiah through their spiritual knowledge. They symbolize all the gentiles (non-Jews) who

search for the truth and find it in Jesus Christ. In early Christian art, they are shown wearing the caps of eastern wise men. Later artists portrayed them as kings representing the three races of humanity. Their names were, according to legend, Balthasar, Caspar, and Melchior.

THE HOLY SPIRIT

Dove. The dove is gentle and pure white. Its hovering motion reminds us of the Holy Spirit's hovering over the waters of the Great Void at the beginning of time, when God created the world out of darkness and chaos. When God overshadowed Jesus in a cloud at his baptism, he said, "This is my Beloved Son." On that occasion, the Holy Spirit descended on Jesus "in bodily form, like a dove," because just as creation occurred as the Spirit hovered over the waters, so now a new creation is beginning in Jesus' willingness to be our Saviour. Jesus, filled with the Holy Spirit, comes as the one who will heal the human race with divine love, and in healing us he will also make a new people, a new family, a new creation of us, in union with himself.

Living Font. This symbol, taken from the hymn "Veni, Creator Spiritus," refers to the association of the Holy Spirit with Baptism. The font at which Baptism is administered is the sa-

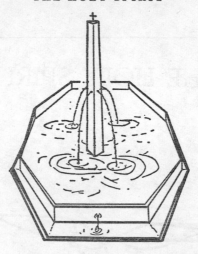

cred space in which the new creation is initiated for each Christian, individually. (See: baptistry, pp. 64, 72.) The waters receive us, and we die sacramentally to the power of sin, and we come up out of the waters newly made alive by the spiritual cleansing that the waters bring about. The waters are empowered to cleanse us spiritually, because they have been blessed by the priest, who breathes on the water in the form of a cross. In Hebrew and Greek, the words for "breath" also mean "spirit." In the consecrating breath of the priest, the Holy Spirit takes possession of the waters so that the new Christian can be spiritually reborn in material that itself is part of the new creation. It is the power of the Holy Spirit that re-creates us, and so we praise the Spirit with the title Fount of Life.

Fire of Charity. The Feast of Pentecost is the "birthday" of the Church, because on that day Mary and the disciples of Jesus were in seclusion, praying and wondering what the future would hold for the followers of Jesus. All of a sudden

(Ac 2), there was a great wind, that is, the presence of the Holy Spirit, and tongue-shaped flames appeared over the heads of the disciples and Mary, the mother of Jesus. The whole group began to praise God in languages that they formerly had not been able to speak. Their praises were heard by people in the streets outside, who wondered what might have happened. The tongues of fire symbolized the presence of the Holy Spirit, filling the disciples with great feelings of love for God and other persons. This "fire of charity" so filled them that they wanted to proclaim the gospel of Jesus to everyone. They were filled with a sense of mission and purpose, and also they finally understood many of the things that Jesus had said during his public ministry that had confused them at the time. Thus love, the central message of Christ, made the disciples worthy to carry on the ministry of the Lord in the world.

Unction (of Spirit). Often the Holy Spirit is symbolized by a container of oil made by crushing olives. This pure vegetable oil was used in the days of the prophets to anoint the head of the king of Israel at his coronation. The head of the High

Priest was also anointed with pure oil. The disciples used oil
to anoint the sick and cure them. And the Church uses oil at
Baptism, Confirmation and Holy Orders as the sign that the
Holy Spirit is present to heal, to restore and to consecrate the
person being baptized, confirmed or ordained. Oil is also used
in the Anointing of the Sick as a sign of both bodily and spiritual healing. The blessing of oil and its use in the sacraments
goes back to the use of oil, to massage sore muscles and to
relax the body, in almost all the ancient civilizations.

The Sevenfold Gift. The seven gifts of the Holy Spirit are
Wisdom, Understanding, Counsel, Fortitude, Knowledge,
Piety, and Fear of the Lord. When the Holy Spirit claims a
human life for God and begins to bring about the new creation in a person, there are definite signs of the Spirit's action.
The person starts to look for ways to please God and to serve
others. The new Christian is eager to study the Scriptures to

learn the ways of God. He or she strives joyfully to overcome temptation. Through frequent prayer, the new Christian learns to listen to the suggestions of God and to reject the thoughts that come from our selfish side. The seven gifts are seven lights on the Christian spiritual path leading to fullness of life in the Kingdom.

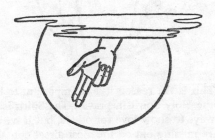

Finger of the Father's Right Hand. If the hand of God is a symbol of God's creating and working in the world, then the finger of God's hardworking "hand" is the most active part of that creative power. The forefinger is the quickest of fingers. It is the pointer; it shows the way. As the forefinger of the hand of God, the Holy Spirit is God's power reaching out to touch each person as directly as possible!

Father of the Poor. Jesus spoke of the Holy Spirit as the "Advocate" that he would send to the apostles. An advocate is someone who helps another person out by advising that person or by speaking out on behalf of that person before his or her opponents. We call lawyers "advocates" because they speak for us in court. The Holy Spirit is "Father" of the poor, because the Spirit takes care of all who are in need. When someone is hungry, the Spirit inspires someone else to see that the hungry one is fed. When someone is lonely, it is the Spirit who suggests to a friend that it is time to visit the

lonely one. This is the reason it is so important to become familiar with the Holy Spirit in prayer. The Spirit is constantly
showing us ways to show love for others, but if we are not listening, we are missing out on the most direct contact between
God and our innermost self. All around the world, people are
crying out for love, for food, for help of many kinds. We
Christians have to decide whether we are going to act to show
God's love for the poor, or whether we are going to continue
to oppress the poor and add to the sufferings of others.

THE CHURCH

Noah's Ark. In the days of the great Flood, God warned Noah to save the living creatures of the earth, and so, reverencing God and showing love for all living things, Noah built an Ark. When the Flood came, Noah's family and the animal families he had gathered were all inside the Ark and were saved from drowning. So, too, the Church gathers us as families in her "ark," to be saved from the powerful waters of bad example and the ways of death. By showing reverence for all persons, for living things and for the good earth that God has given us, we are united in our hearts to God himself. As members of the Church, we show by our lives that we believe in a loving God, who made the world out of love and who wants to share his goodness with us.

Table. It is not the table itself, but the human action at the table that gives it a symbolic meaning. The family gathers, a prayer of thanks is offered to God, the meal is blessed, and all partake joyfully and eagerly. The hungry family is fed, and as the meal goes on a word is shared, a thought, a feeling, an idea, a smile, or a frown. The children are taught good manners: to listen attentively, speak clearly, use knife, fork, and spoon correctly; questions are asked and answered, and the things that happened to the family that day are told.

So, too, the Table of the Lord is a gathering place for the family, the "new family" of those who believe in the Lord Jesus. Eagerly, we listen to the stories of the Bible. Jesus, the apostles, the prophets and kings are all part of our family, and we want to come to know them better. We are taught how to live well, how to seek God in all things, and Jesus himself explains the meaning of everything by coming to us as food in the Holy Eucharist. He breaks open the bread at the table, and is himself our bread. He pours a cup of wine for us, and he is himself the wine. He invites us to listen, to be grateful for his presence, and to be changed. Who would not become someone different, someone new, at his table?

Fountain of Life. The first of all fountains is that in the Garden of Eden, from which the four rivers at the center of the earth spring forth. But the greatest fountain, of which the fountain of Eden is the prototype, is Jesus himself. He said: " 'If anyone thirst, let him come to me. . . .' As Scripture

says: 'From his breast shall flow fountains of living water.'"
(Jn 7:37–39). Also, when the soldiers pierced his side, a flow
of blood and water came forth. Jesus on the cross became
a fountain, and the Church is refreshed in that fountain. In
the sacraments, we receive the graces that were set loose in
the world by the death and Resurrection of Jesus. In baptism,
we are washed in the river from the side of Christ. In the
Eucharist, we drink of the Blood of Christ. We ourselves, in
our bodies, are fountains of living waters—the blood flowing
constantly and being renewed by fresh air in our lungs and
in the nourishment of food. Our gratitude to God for air,
water and food leads us to listen more closely for the nearness
of Jesus, who invites us to come home to the Father through
the sacraments of the Church.

The Lamp. Jesus often speaks of lamps: the oil lamps of the
Five Wise Virgins and the Five Foolish Virgins, the lamp that
should be on a stand and not hidden under a bushel. Today,
with electric light, it is not easy to imagine that all indoor
lighting was once by candle or oil lamp. The lamp flame,
small, smoky and dim, slowly consuming the oil and the linen
wick, was a symbol of many things: of the energy of a per-

son's life burning brightly at first but little by little weakening, using up its strength until there is old age and death. But in the Bible the lamp and its light come to symbolize the Light of the World, God's Word, who became a man, Jesus. The Word can be read by lamplight, but the Saviour is himself both Word and Light. He explains by his actions what and who he is for us. Thus, we light the Paschal candle at Easter, carving the cross, the nails and the numerals of the year into the wax that the bees make. The new fire of Easter, symbolizing the rising of Christ, is used to light the candlewick, and the deacon proclaims, "Christ, our Light!" and we respond:

"Thanks be to God!" Thus Christ comes once again to life in our midst, in the midst of the Church, the faithful, gathered together in the sight of God. The Resurrection occurs once again in the world of suffering (the cross), the world of time (the year numerals carved in wax), the world of beauty (candle wax made by bees from the nectar of flowers), the world of eternity (Alpha and Omega are carved into the candle—the beginning and the end of all time), and Jesus comes as Light, as a new fire that makes everything different, because he shows that everything that exists proclaims a message of love from God to us.

The Orante. Who was she—this stately woman at prayer, painted on the walls of the catacombs, the underground burial vaults of ancient Rome? She came to symbolize the Church at prayer. This one woman stands for the new family of believers gathered together by the message of Jesus about God's special love for us. This new family, though persecuted

and blessed with martyrs, still prays for the world, still hopes for the salvation of all the human race, still hopes for peace and justice for all.

The Woman. The Church was portrayed as a woman at prayer or carrying her Child, the Child Christ, who is coming into the world. This is Mother Church, who nurtures all of us with faith, hope and love. Sitting at her feet, we listen to her as she tells us the stories of Jesus, the ways of God among us. Mother Church is also the Bride, the beautiful young woman awaiting the return of her husband-to-be, that is, she is the Church of which we are all a part, the community that prays together, breaks bread together, and awaits the coming of Christ in glory.

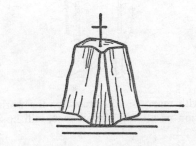

Holy Mountain. Hills, mountains and other high places are strong symbols of the relationship of God and humans. The mountaintop is the place of meeting with God. Moses met God on Mount Sinai; Jesus taught "on the mount" and was transfigured on the mount. To climb the mountain requires effort: There is a struggle against our own weight and the steepness of the incline. But once on top, we feel weightless, our eyes wander freely across the countryside over great distances. The sky and clouds feel closer somehow. We are still on earth, but the heavens seem so much more open. We breathe deeply and receive the clean feeling of the presence of the Spirit of God. The mountaintop is the favored place for Benedictine monasteries; many shrines and churches are on mountaintops, because these high places keep alive in us the experience of meeting God at those places where heaven and earth seem to touch. Jesus died on the cross on the mount Golgotha (also called Calvary)—the place where sins and failures meet God's forgiveness. Every church, every altar, and every Christian is a Calvary, where we meet God on the mount of our heart and find forgiveness and love.

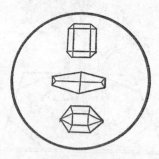

Precious Stones. (Ex 19–31; 28:9–12, 17–21) "Two onyx stones of the ephod on which were written the names of the Twelve Tribes for remembrance."

The breastplate of the High Priest had four rows of stones, each engraved like a signet with the name of one of the twelve sons of Israel. The stones were sardius, topaz, carbuncle, emerald, sapphire, diamond, jacinth, agate, amethyst, beryl, onyx, jasper. Precious stones! Glittering in the eye and sending penetrating light into the depths of the mind—for "remembrance" of how precious in the eyes of the Lord are his holy people, the children of Israel, and the Church. Just as we remember God's love for us in the sight of the precious stones on the vestments of the High Priest, so, too, God looks on us and "remembers" his love for us. For we are God's precious stones, and the most precious is Jesus. When God looks upon Jesus, who sits "at the right hand of God," he cannot help but think of us humans. Jesus is forever our mediator with the Father, the channel of God's grace to us; he is the Cornerstone of the Kingdom of God. Out of that Cornerstone, and out of the precious stones that we are, God is fashioning the new Jerusalem in the Book of Revelation, whose walls are built with the same gemstones that are listed above, and on whose foundations are the names of the Twelve Apostles of the Lamb (Rv 21:2–3, also 12–21).

Paradise. The Paradise Tree. St. Gregory of Nyssa once said that the Church is planted as a paradise in this world. We ought to be like that first garden that the Lord planted in Eden—fresh, pure and alive. But the world in which we are planted is a world of struggle, and we are part of that struggle.

The tree of the garden and its forbidden fruit, "of the knowledge of good and evil," symbolize our disobedience, by which disorder came into the world. Every generation fights a battle: the battle to either obey or disobey God. Disobedience is so common that it is more than we can do to be as obedient as we would like to be. Sin is passed on year after year as persons choose to reach out for the fruit in a gesture of greed. But the fruit of that same mysterious tree would not be poison if we were willing to receive it in due time from the hand of God, and if we were willing then to share it with others.

The Church is that new family planted in this world that labors to cultivate a new garden, a new paradise, in which the good fruit of Jesus Christ will grow. In the sacraments, we partake of the nourishing spiritual food that Jesus offers: himself. He gives us his very self, and by partaking of his Body and Blood, we are made not only his servants in working in the garden, but we also become his friends for eternity.

Tree of Life. This is the tree that foreshadows the cross. It was planted in the mystical Garden of Paradise as the tree of wisdom, and it tells us the secret of how to live.

The tree starts small, with a tiny seed; it grows in the earth, sending roots farther and farther into the ground. At the same time, it reaches out into the air and sunlight with its branches. When it is full-grown it can produce fruit, a little at first but soon a great abundance. The Church, too, started with a small number. Its founder, Jesus Christ, died and was buried, like the seed that falls to the ground. But the seed germinates, rises from the earth, and so did the Church, growing wider and stronger in storms and persecutions, reaching in ever so many ways to receive the sunlight of God's grace and the living waters at its roots. Our community puts its roots down in the roots of God's tree of life; beneath the boughs of this tree we can grow. We may eat the fruit of this tree and find ourselves healed by the power of the sacraments; we enjoy the cool shade of this tree, and we see it as a ladder to heaven that we can climb in the company of the angels.

St. Peter's Ship, or Bark. Since so many of the first apostles were fishermen, it should be no surprise that the Church was often symbolized as a ship. A ship can "walk on water." A ship is in the hands of God, especially in a storm. And with a good man at the helm, the passengers and cargo are safe. So Jesus appointed Peter to be his helmsman, Peter "the rock." "You are Peter and on this rock I will build my Church. And the gates of the underworld can never hold out against it. I will give you the keys of the kingdom of heaven" (Mt 16:18–19).

MARY

Monogram: MARIA. Here we have a good example of the playful hand of the artist giving praise to God. The mother of Jesus, Mary, was graced more than any other human person. Thus we say, "Hail, Mary, full of grace," in the words of the Angel Gabriel when he announced that she would become the mother of God. This name, Mary, or Maria (Miriam, in Hebrew), is full of beautiful sounds that are themselves consoling and harmonious to our ears. Her name should be among the holy sounds, along with the holy names of Jesus and Yahweh. The beautiful sound Maria can be made into a sacred monogram or sign. Can you find all the letters in these examples?

Mirror of Justice. Ancient peoples were fascinated by mirrors and by the marvelous ability of glass, water and polished metal to reflect the human face. Surely there is something magical in a mirror; perhaps inside the mirror there is a portion of our soul that takes our shape and calls us to itself. The mirror became a topic for much imaginative fantasy. But how is Mary a mirror? In her life, Mary obeyed God completely and loved God totally. Even when she did not fully understand, she trusted. She wanted, more than anything else, to see God's will done. Mary reflects God's justice in the world. She so perfectly reflected God's intentions and his justice that the Son of God was formed in her. Jesus, perfect image of the Father, was formed in the pure mirror of Mary's heart.

Seat of Wisdom. Mary's wisdom came from her meditation on the Scriptures. By her study of God's word, she learned how to do the will of God. When we see the Child Jesus sitting on Mary's lap, we see Wisdom enthroned. Jesus, the Wisdom of God, by whom all things were made, is seated on the perfect throne, Mary, who presents him to the world.

Ark of the Covenant. In the days of Moses, the stone tablets on which the Commandments were written by God were carried in an ark. The ark was lifted by strong men holding the ends of golden poles. Golden cherubim held their wings over the center of the ark, showing reverence for the presence of God. Mary, too, was an ark, carrying in her womb the new Covenant of friendship between God and humans. This Covenant is a Person, Jesus, truly divine and truly human. Each Christian imitates Mary by carrying Jesus in his or her heart. Like Mary, we strive to bring the Jesus within us into the light of day, into our daily thoughts, words and deeds.

Mystical Rose. Something mystical is something silent, a deep secret that one must approach very quietly, as if it were a deer in the forest. If we come close too quickly, it hears us and springs away. This rose that we call Mary is a mysterious rose, a hidden rose. It is Mary's quiet trust in God. As all the events of Jesus' life unfolded before her, Mary kept them in her heart, pondering over everything that God was doing in her divine Son. This quiet reflection in Mary's heart is the bud of the rose. As Mary's understanding grew, the bud began to open up. The mysteries of the rosary take us through this rose as it opens up to its full beauty when Mary is made Queen of Heaven and Queen of all the saints.

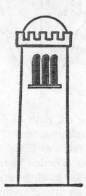

Tower of David, Tower of Ivory. These symbols of beauty and strength show us the true strength of Mary and of all Christians. Our strength is God alone, who made King David strong, courageous and beautiful as pure white ivory. King David was not always strong. He often sinned and failed to do as God commanded. But in the midst of his sins, he would see how weak he had become in relying on himself alone, and he would repent and turn back to God. Mary, as a descendant of King David, inherited his virtues but not his faults. By letting God be the strength to support her weakness, she was made strong enough to be a mother for all of us.

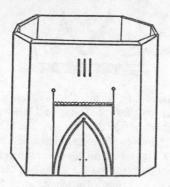

Gate of Heaven. Mary's openness and obedience made it possible for God to become man in Jesus Christ. Mary was chosen to be the "doorway" into our world for the power of God. For us, Mary is the way also. She listened to God's word and she lived God's word. She brought Christ into the world not only physically but spiritually. Every one of us, by faithfulness and love, can do just what she did spiritually. We, too, can become gates of heaven through which God's grace can flow to others, to the extent that we, like Mary, allow Christ to fill us.

Morning Star. When Mary was born, it was as if a bright morning star had appeared in the glow of a coming dawn. The angels knew already that her birth would be the first signal that Christ, too, would soon be coming. Mary, the "Morning Star," is a symbol of Advent, that time of joyful waiting for the coming of Jesus Christ the Lord.

Queen of Heaven. Mary is so often spoken of as the model Christian. She is mother of Jesus and also mother of the Church. The highest honor that crowns her life is her coronation as Queen of Heaven. She presides over all the saints and angels; she is the highest of all God's creatures. In her loving obedience and cooperation with the will of God, she fulfilled all the prophecies and hopes of ancient times. She became the new Eve, mother of a new human family, the Church of Jesus Christ.

Immaculate Heart. "Thine own soul a sword shall pierce." These mysterious words were spoken to Mary by the wise Simeon when Mary and Joseph presented Jesus in the Temple in Jerusalem. Simeon knew in advance that Mary would have to suffer alongside her son in order that the new Covenant may be established. He knew she would be faithful to the end, even to the point of standing at the foot of the cross while Jesus died. Most of all, he knew that her heart was already pierced by another sword, the two-edged sword of the word of God in Holy Scripture. Because she was strong in her love of Scripture, she was prepared for all that would happen to her. Knowing the word of God in the Bible, she was ready in the depth of her heart to be united to the Word of God in the flesh, Jesus Christ.

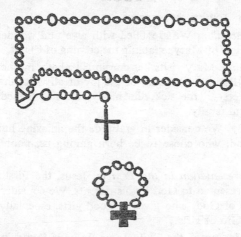

Rosary. The rosary is a method of meditating on the life of Jesus through the eyes of Mary. We are invited to hear the word of God and keep it, as Mary did. We are encouraged to join Mary, who pondered over the life of Jesus in her pure and devoted heart. And we are called to join the unfolding of the mystical rose of Mary's holiness in our own lives.

The method is easy. A set of rosary beads is used. On the crucifix, pray the Apostles' Creed. Then move your hand to the next bead, and pray the Our Father, then three Hail Mary's, and on the fifth bead above the cross, say the Glory Be to the Father. Next, form a picture in your imagination of the first "mystery," or sacred event, of the rosary meditation. This is the Announcement (Annunciation) by the Angel Gabriel that Mary would become the mother of the Saviour. Say one Our Father, then pray ten Hail Mary's, counting on the first set of beads, and conclude the first meditation with the Glory Be to the Father. Keep the image of Mary and the Angel gratefully before the inner eye of your imagination. Continue to meditate on each set of ten beads in the same way. Each set corresponds to a different sacred event, or mystery:

THE FIVE JOYFUL MYSTERIES

1. *Annunciation.* We are filled with awe and wonder at the openness of Mary, enabling the coming of Christ.

2. *Visitation.* Mary visits her cousin Elizabeth, mother of John the Baptist. We think of the joy of all visits shared by believers—to the sick, the needy, the imprisoned, to friends and family.

3. *Nativity.* We consider in gratitude the amazing humility of God, who chose to be born among us, poor and helpless.

4. *The Presentation in the Temple.* Jesus, the Firstborn Son, is presented to God by his parents. We consider the goodness of God, who gives us good gifts, especially his Son, the Gift of gifts.

5. *The Finding of the Child Jesus.* Jesus is found in the Temple discussing Scripture with the rabbis and teachers. We consider how determined Jesus was to learn about the mission his Father had given him. We consider the calling that God is offering in *our* lives.

THE FIVE SORROWFUL MYSTERIES

1. *The Agony in the Garden.* Jesus is tormented in spirit in the garden just before his arrest. We consider the difficulties in following Christ, and we ask his help in our struggle to be faithful.

2. *The Scourging at the Pillar.* Jesus is chained to a stone pillar and beaten. We consider how an easy life can weaken our determination to obey God's will.

3. *The Crowning with Thorns.* Jesus' head is wounded by a twisted cap of thorns. He is mocked as "king" by the soldiers. We consider that standing up for the truth often leads to humiliation, and we pray for courage.

4. *The Carrying of the Cross.* Jesus carries the instrument of his own death on his back. We consider his words: "If anyone would be my disciple, let him [or her] take up his [or her] cross daily and follow me."

5. *The Crucifixion.* Jesus is nailed to the cross. After hanging for three hours, he dies. We consider how total and final a reality is death. Can we give ourselves as fully to *life* as Jesus gave himself to *us* by dying?

THE FIVE GLORIOUS MYSTERIES

1. *The Resurrection.* Jesus rises from the dead. We consider the hope that each of us has in the great and small crucifixions of our lives, that we will rise again through faith in the Risen Christ.

2. *Ascension.* The whole universe is filled with the presence of the Risen Christ. We consider our own future with Jesus and the Father and the Holy Spirit in eternal life.

3. *The Descent of the Holy Spirit.* Mary and the disciples of Jesus are filled with a sense of mission by the gift of the Holy Spirit in the form of flames of divine fire. We pray for the grace to live the Christian life fully.

4. *The Assumption of Mary.* Mary is taken up into the life of God after her death. We consider that her total union with Jesus is our own destiny; as Mary was raised, so shall we be raised into eternal life.

5. *The Coronation of Mary.* Mary is received by Jesus and made Queen of Heaven, and of all the saints, because her love of God made possible the coming of salvation. We consider the power of love to change the world.

THE SAINTS

The followers of Jesus whose names and stories have become a cherished part of the Catholic faith are the saints. The holy angels, the prophets and kings of ancient Israel, Mary, Elizabeth, Joseph and John the Baptist, the apostles, the martyrs, virgins and monks, the great teachers and visionaries, the humble working folk, the founders of religious orders, the missionaries, are all found among the saints. The saints are commemorated at Mass usually on the day of their death, that is, their "heavenly birthday." Knowing the symbols of the saints is the best way to recognize them in stained-glass windows, in stone carvings, or mosaics in churches around the world. Usually a saint's symbol is derived from an event in his or her life or in the manner of his or her death. There are other reasons for the origin of a symbol. St. Agnes, a famous virgin and martyr, has one of the oldest symbols for a saint: a lamb, because her name means "lamb" in Latin. St. Hugh, a monk and bishop of the Middle Ages, was followed at all times by a wild swan, so his symbol is a swan.

The stories of the saints have been told in many ways by the master storytellers of the Church. Very often, the fanciful legends of the saints provide us with the symbols that we associate with the most popular saints.

Here is a selection from the thousands of saints and their symbols:

St. Ambrose. Beehive, symbolizes his hard work in building up the Church.

St. Andrew. A cross shaped like the letter X, on which he was crucified.

St. Anthony, Abbot. A pig, a bell, and a T-shaped cross. He was a hermit (symbolized by the T cross), and his followers raised pigs during the Middle Ages.

St. Anthony of Padua. He was a Franciscan friar, holding a lily of purity and the Child Jesus. Noted for his chastity and his closeness to Christ.

St. Apollonia. Dental pliers, with which all her teeth were pulled out by her torturers in their attempt to get her to renounce Christ.

St. Augustine. The heart, because he taught the love of God. Also shown with miter, crosier, and many books, because he was a bishop and great theologian.

St. Barbara. A tower, because she was imprisoned in a brass tower.

St. Bartholomew. A great knife, because he was skinned alive. The great Italian artist Michelangelo painted him holding his own skin in "The Last Judgment," in the Sistine Chapel, in Rome.

St. Benedict. A raven, a cross, a broken cup or a crosier. A raven carried off a loaf of poisoned bread that a wicked person had given the saint; his cross is powerful against demons; a poisoned cup broke when he blessed it; he is patriarch of the monks of the Catholic Church.

St. Bernardino of Siena. The monogram of the Holy Name of Jesus (IHS). This was his favorite subject for preaching.

St. Catherine. A wheel, because this great philosopher-saint was tortured on a spiked wheel.

St. Cecilia. Harp or organ pipes. She is patron of music and musicians, because she loved to sing the praises of God.

St. Clare. She holds a pyx containing the Eucharistic Bread, which she used to frighten off invaders trying to break into her convent.

St. Denis. A bishop, holding his severed head in his hands. According to legend, not even beheading could stop his missionary activities.

St. Dominic. Robed in black and white and holding the rosary that was given to him by Our Lady, according to legend. Also, he is symbolized by a gray or white dog, because the Dominican Order is the "watchdog" of the Lord (Latin: *domini canes* = The Lord's dogs).

St. Francis of Assisi. Has the Five Wounds of Christ (the Stigmata) on his body, which he received in a vision of the crucified Christ on Mount Alvernia. He is also shown preaching to the birds or calming a wild wolf. He founded the Franciscans.

St. George. A knight slaying a dragon, according to his legend.

St. Giles. A doe. He sheltered her from hunters in his forest hermitage.

St. Helena. A cross, because she found the True Cross of Jesus, buried on Mount Calvary (Golgotha), just outside Jerusalem.

St. Hubert and St. Eustace. Hunters who met Christ in a vision of his Cross, seen between the antlers of a stag.

St. Ignatius Loyola. The IHS monogram in a solar disk, with the motto: "For the Greater Glory of God." He founded the Society of Jesus (Jesuit Fathers).

St. James the Greater. A pilgrim, wearing a large hat and cape. On his sack, there is the famous scallop shell that represented the wandering of pilgrims from shrine to shrine in Europe in the Middle Ages.

St. Jerome. A lion at his feet (according to a mistaken but popular legend that he had a pet lion); also, a cardinal's red hat, because Pope St. Damasus commissioned him to translate the Bible into Latin from the original Hebrew and Greek.

St. John the Baptist. He holds the labarum of the Resurrection and points to the Lamb of God. He is the "forerunner" of Jesus Christ.

St. Joseph. Lily of purity, or a T-square symbolizing his trade (he was a carpenter).

St. Jude. A sailing ship, symbolizing his missionary journeys. Often shown with the flame of the Holy Spirit over his head.

King David. Harp, on which he played while singing the Psalms he wrote.

St. Lawrence. A deacon in a dalmatic, holding an iron grill, on which he was roasted to death, according to legend.

St. Louis. The fleur-de-lis. He was the King of France and a crusader. He brought the crown of thorns to Paris and built a chapel to enshrine it, out of devotion to the sufferings of Jesus.

St. Lucy. A lamp (*lucia* means light in Latin) or eyes in a dish because her eyes were put out during her martyrdom, according to legend. Like all the martyrs, she holds a palm of victory.

St. Martin. A soldier cutting his cloak in two and giving half to a beggar, who turns out to be Jesus "in disguise."

St. Nicholas. Three sacks of gold or three golden balls, symbols of the gifts he gave to three poor children while they slept.

St. Patrick. Three-leafed clover, because he used the clover leaf to explain the Trinity to his Irish converts.

St. Paul the Apostle. A two-edged sword, because he was inspired by the Holy Spirit both to preach and to write the word of God.

St. Peter. Keys of the Kingdom, given to him by Christ.

St. Scholastica. A dove. According to legend, her twin brother, St. Benedict, saw her soul ascend to heaven like a dove after her death.

St. Sebastian. Arrows. He is portrayed as a young soldier executed for his faith by a "firing squad" armed with bows and arrows.

St. Thomas Aquinas. Dominican friar with an eye and a golden solar disk over his heart. Symbol of God the Father, the Source of his teaching and the Object of his loving contemplation.

St. Vincent Ferrer. Holds the rosary of St. Dominic, wears the black-and-white habit, and has angel's wings, because he was called "The Angel of the Judgment." He often preached on the coming of Christ in glory at the end of time—the Last Judgment.

ANGELS

The Archangels Gabriel, Michael, Raphael and Uriel.

Michael is an armored angel holding the scales of justice.

Gabriel is white-robed and holds a lily of purity, because he announced the birth of Christ to the Virgin Mary.

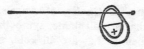

Raphael holds a sword or a staff and a traveling bag. He is the guardian of travelers and healer of the sick.

Uriel, "the Fire of God," holds the flaming sword at the gate of the Garden of Eden.

The Nine Orders, or Choirs, of Angels. Seraphim are six-winged beings that are all flame, symbolizing love. Cherubim are six-winged beings that are all gold, symbolizing wisdom. Thrones are scarlet wheels with many eyes—the chariot of God—symbolizing judgment.

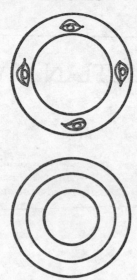

Dominions, Virtues and Powers are responsible for the movement of the Divine Will through the stars and planets. Principalities, Archangels and Angels communicate the will of God to nations, cities and individuals on earth.

CHRISTIAN LIVING

The River of Grace. Imagine a wide river flowing with clear, bubbling water, its banks lined with trees heavy with fruit and abundant green leaves. The sunlight sparkles in the waves. The river is a mighty symbol of God's grace, his generosity, overflowing and never drying up. Think of all the good things that come from a river: Its fish give us food, its waters are traveled by boats, you can swim by its shores, it waters the fields and orchards, it cools the hot summer countryside, and even when it freezes, the river has a special power and beauty. In the Bible there are many rivers: the four rivers of Paradise, each of them springing up at the mystical center of the world, the starting point of God's creative work; the Nile, which turns to blood when Pharaoh disobeys God's word spoken through Moses; the Jordan, which the Israelites crossed over into the Promised Land. The Jordan was made especially holy when John the Baptist plunged Jesus into its pure waters. There are also rivers of vision, such as the river of promise that Isaiah saw pouring prosperity over the city of Jerusalem as a sign of God's abundant forgiveness and unfailing love. And there is the river of blood and water flowing from the side of Christ on the cross, which symbolizes the grace of the sacraments of Baptism and Eucharist, which we receive from the heart of the Church.

The Seven Sacraments. It has been said that Jesus, by showing us in his life and teachings what the love of God is for us, is a sacrament of the Father. The Church, in showing us Jesus and uniting us to him, is the sacrament of Christ. And the seven sacraments of the Church are the specific fountains of grace by which Christians enter the abundant life of God, the life-force that transforms our existence in this world. Seven has been a number with symbolic meaning for a long time in human history. It seems most often to stand for perfection, for completeness. Often, one is expected to pass through seven gates or seven fortresses in order to attain a goal in fairy tales and legends. The skies were thought to be divided into seven layers, ruled by the seven Spirits, or Powers, represented by the Sun, the Moon, Mercury, Venus, Mars, Jupiter and Saturn. The seven sacraments seem to represent the completeness of life in the Church, since they focus on beginnings and endings, healing, and deciding, along the way to the Father.

Baptism: This sacrament is our initiation into the Christian community by water and the gift of the Holy Spirit. Baptism means "a washing," and it is done in a font, or baptistry, by immersion or sprinkling with pure, blessed water. The new Christian is given a candle lit from the great Paschal candle, inscribed at the Easter Vigil with the signs and symbols of the year of grace. Thus, water, the font, and a Paschal candle—all may be used to symbolize Baptism.

Confirmation: This sacrament completes the initiation begun in Baptism by the anointing with holy oil by the bishop, to symbolize the gifts of the Holy Spirit that will enable the adult Christian to persevere in the life in Christ Jesus. The symbols of Confirmation are the Dove of the Holy Spirit, the flame of Pentecost, the flask of oil, and the bishop's miter.

Eucharist: This word means "thanksgiving," and it is in this greatest of sacraments that we offer thanks for all the good things that God has done and is doing and will do for us. It is the gospel in action. In the Eucharist, we receive the true Body and Blood of Jesus Christ—under the forms of bread and wine. Just as Jesus gave himself to his apostles at the Last Supper, this Most Blessed Sacrament is a continuation of Jesus' presence with us. Since we receive him as food, we are reminded that he has invited us to follow him to

the heavenly banquet in eternity, in the love he shares with our Father, the Lord of the Universe. There is no limit to the prayers, insights, reflections and joys that come to the believer through this sacrament. This is something for you to explore for yourself. The symbols of the Eucharist are the simple cup and loaf, or grapes and wheat, or sometimes just the holy table on which the bread and wine are offered in sacrifice in union with Christ to God our Father.

Penance (the Sacrament of Reconciliation): In this sacrament, the pilgrims, you and I, receive directly, for our particular sins and offenses, the total forgiveness of God. So great is the love between the Father and the Son, Jesus, that any sin can be forgiven if the believer comes to this sacrament with a sincere heart and a willingness to turn away from sin. This sacrament is full of the joy of knowing that Jesus has already done the work for us; all that is asked of us is that we accept the love of God for us every day of our lives. The symbols of this sacrament are the gesture of forgiveness offered by the priest, and the Keys given by Christ to Peter, which open and shut the way to the Kingdom of God.

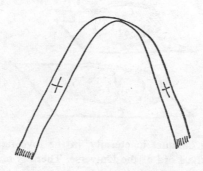

Holy Orders: This is the sacrament by which a Christian is called to serve his fellow believers as a deacon, priest or bishop. It is a sacrament of decision, since it is given only once and it transforms one's whole way of life. Through this sacrament, all the others are given to the Christian community, and the gifts given by Christ to the apostles continue to be handed down by the laying on of hands. Only a bishop can ordain priests and deacons. Bishops are consecrated by several bishops. This great sacrament is symbolized by the Dove of the Holy Spirit, who consecrates the priest; the oil of the Holy Spirit (chrism), which is used to ordain; or by the symbols of priesthood, the stole and the chalice.

Matrimony: This is the sacrament by which a man and a woman pledge to give their lives into each other's hands, and so they exchange rings as a symbol of their love and union. In this union, the love of two human beings is perfected by the grace of Christ, who enables them to live together and to bring up children who will continue the work of God that

began in creation and was made new and holy by the coming of Christ. Matrimony looks forward to the life of the future in the Kingdom of God, where all will be united in an eternal love. The harmony that the Holy Spirit brings to marriage is sometimes symbolized by a musical instrument.

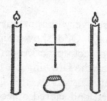

Anointing of the Sick: In this sacrament, holy oil is used to bless the body of a sick person. The purpose is twofold: The sick person may get physically well by the grace of the sacrament, and also the sick person is given spiritual healing by the power of God. This anointing with oil and blessing reminds us that in both life and death we belong to the Lord, and that our bodies are holy to the Lord, and finally, that the Lord has extended to his followers the power to heal. The symbols of the Anointing of the Sick are the flask of oil, a pair of candles, and the labarum of the Resurrection.

You will notice that among the physical things needed for the sacraments are bread, wine, water and oil. Each of these ordinary things is a product of the earth. Purest of all is water, but even water must be held in a basin or font made by human hands. Oil must be pressed out of the fruit of the olive, and wine must be squeezed out of the grapes and allowed to ferment. Bread comes from wheat, grown in fields and on hillsides, ground up in the mill, mixed with yeast and water to make dough, kneaded into bread, formed into loaves and baked slowly and carefully. Each of the materials needed for the sacraments is a gift of God coming to us through the earth. And each material requires human effort to be used. God's grace, too, comes freely from God, and we are grateful for the love and sustenance that grace is for us. But grace has no effect in ourselves or in our world unless we work with it. God provides everything we need, but if we do nothing, the gifts of God fade away. Jesus warned us: "From those to whom much has been given, much will be expected." The sacraments are the perfect signs of our cooperation with God's intentions in this world.

Sacramentals are also very important in showing us the many very special ways God shows himself to us. A sacramental is a blessed object, practice, or rite which may aid us in our spiritual growth. Drawing on the spiritual power of the united prayers of Christians, the Church makes use of various rituals, prayers, and sacred objects to extend the blessings of God in the world. Some examples of sacramentals include: the rosary, holy water, blessed candles, the Advent wreath, blessing-prayers for homes, vestments, medals, and chalices. There are easily hundreds of sacramentals in the use and tradition of the Catholic Church.

The Palm. "The just one flourishes like the palm tree and grows like the Lebanon cedar." Those persons who receive the Lord with joy are blessed with growth in "wisdom, strength and grace." The palm is a symbol of growth and of hope. It is the sign of victory over the weaknesses that hold us back from following Jesus with our whole hearts. The palm was once the sign of the pilgrim; it reminded all he met that the pilgrim had been to the holy city of Jerusalem and had glimpsed the places where Jesus had taught, died and rose

from the dead. On Palm Sunday, we celebrate Jesus' entry into Jerusalem by waving palms in procession in church, and so say our "yes" in public to our willingness to follow Jesus even to the cross. The palm is thus also a symbol of the martyrs.

Ashes, Ash Wednesday. Ashes have been a sign of penance since the days of the Hebrew prophets. Job put ashes on his head when he felt abandoned by God. When Jonah preached to the pagan folk of Nineveh, even they put ashes on their heads and the heads of their animals, to show how they were sorry for their sins. But Jesus has a warning for us when we put on ashes to make the appearance of sorrow and repentance. He reminds us that repentance is first of all a matter of the heart, and a mere public show of sorrow is meaningless unless we really change our lives. The Hebrew prophets also warned us that the deeds of social justice, righting wrongs, correcting inequities, getting rid of poverty and prejudice are far better signs of penance in the sight of God than wearing ashes and fasting. Christians dare to put on ashes only as an outward sign of an inward conversion of life that bears fruit in deeds of justice and compassion.

The Two-edged Sword, the Sword of the Spirit. The word of God in Holy Scripture is referred to as a sword. It is two-edged because it cuts whichever way it is used; both the speaker and the hearer must respond to God's word. And it is the Spirit's sword because it is the weapon of compassion that God uses to touch the human heart.

The Scriptures read at Mass are set in order in a book called the *Lectionary,* which means "book of readings." Because we meet the Lord in his written word, this book or any Bible is a "sacramental," that is, an instrument of grace. The Bible is always handled reverently and cared for with special attention. The Lectionary for Mass should be carried with full attention to its sacramental importance. The binding of this book should be especially strong and beautiful, to remind us visibly of the sacred meaning within.

Gold, Frankincense and myrrh. These three gifts given by the Magi to the Child Jesus have always symbolized kingship, priesthood and the sufferings of Christ. Gold is always used in ornament and jewelry to represent the Kingdom of God. Saints have golden halos in art to show that they fully belong to the Kingdom. Frankincense (or incense) is a special mixture of fragrant wood chips, sap droplets and perfumes that produces a fragrant smoke when burned on a piece of charcoal in a "thurible," or censer. This smoke rising from the censer is a symbol of the prayers of Christians rising to the heavens into the "sight" of God. Myrrh is an ointment made from the resin of a tree, often mixed with an oily substance, also from a tree. It is dark red or brown and has a pungent, bitter aroma; it was used in perfume. Its bitterness and color remind us of the suffering and death of Jesus, but this material is very rare and is not used in the Catholic liturgy.

You can get an idea of what these resinous materials are from the droplets of sap on cherry and pine trees. Try burning some of this sap on charcoal as an experiment.

Church, Basilica Form. The ancient basilicas (basilica means "the king's building") were used by the Roman emperors as lawcourts. When Emperor Constantine became a Christian, he donated several basilicas to the Church, and

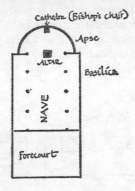

constructed others, to be used for places of worship. Unlike older temples, which had large courtyards for the lay folk and very small, walled-in sanctuaries for the priests only, in the wide Christian basilicas everyone could see the actions of the priest at the altar. All the faithful are included in the worship of God. The basilica is a sacramental because it represents the "House of God." It gathers the whole people of God under one roof. Its floor plan shows the relationships of all parts of the Christian family to one another and makes it possible for all to come to hear the word of God and share the Eucharist together. The church or basilica became so closely associated with the community gathered within it that people almost forgot that "the Church" is not a building; the Church is the people of God.

In the main basilica of a city, the bishop presides at Mass. His chair is called a "cathedra," and his basilica is called the "cathedral" of the diocese. The cathedral is the central and most important church in each diocese. Have you ever visited your cathedral?

Baptistry. Early Christians constructed an octagonal building next to their cathedral. Inside the octagon was a pool of water into which a person could descend and ascend by two sets of steps. In this building, on the night of Holy Saturday, new Christians were baptized by the bishop of the town. The

Baptistry

eight sides represented the six days of creation, plus the seventh day, the Sabbath, plus the "Eighth Day," the day of the Resurrection of Jesus, on which the world was spiritually recreated and the human race gifted with salvation. The pool is a sign of the fountain of life in Paradise, the source and center of all the waters of the world. This pool is the source of sacramental grace given in Baptism. Four fonts, or spouts, were set in the walls of the pool, representing the four rivers of Paradise. The octagon represents the union of heaven and earth in the new creation: Heaven, a circle, is combined with the symbol of the earth, a square. The earth was not literally thought of as square (many people in ancient and medieval times knew that the earth is round). The square is a good symbol of the earth, because the earth is our home, and houses in most parts of the earth are built in the form of a square or rectangle. Thus we speak of "the four corners of the world."

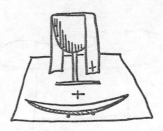

Vessels Used at Mass. Mass Linens. The objects used to celebrate the Eucharist gained symbolic meaning in people's imaginations, as is perfectly understandable. Something that we consider valuable and holy becomes the source of many legends and stories as we consider the wonderful things that

God has done in the world. For example, there is the story of the Holy Grail, the cup used by Jesus at the Last Supper. In the Middle Ages, knights would go off in search of this holy cup, which is actually a symbol of salvation and the fullness of life. Today, artists have tried to make the chalice and paten used to hold the wine and bread at Eucharist as simple and large as possible. The idea is to make the pure symbol as clear as possible. Older patens were just a small disk of gold or silver. Today, we use larger loaves of bread in the liturgy, so larger patens are used. Often, beautiful and simple chalices and patens of ceramic materials are used instead of gold and silver. Patens are, in some churches, being replaced with large baskets, finely woven, to hold the Eucharistic bread.

The Purificator is a small linen cloth draped over the chalice and used to wipe the chalice and for the priest to dry his fingers.

The pall, burse and chalice veil are rarely used today. The pall is a square of stiffened linen placed over the chalice; the burse is a pocket of stiff embroidered cloth into which the linen cloth called the corporal (used under the chalice and paten on the altar) is placed before and after use. The chalice veil, also an embroidered cloth made in the correct liturgical color, is placed over the chalice, pall and paten before and after mass.

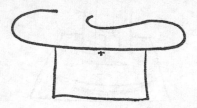

Priest's Vestments.

Amice: A square of white linen wrapped around the neck and covering the shoulders. It symbolizes the "helmet of salvation," the virtue of hope in St. Paul's First Epistle to the Thessalonians (5:8). It is the priest's strength in overcoming the assaults of the Evil One.

Alb: A long white garment, originally of linen, reaching from the neck to the feet. It symbolizes innocence and purity (alb means "white," the color of purity), required of all who minister to the Lord.

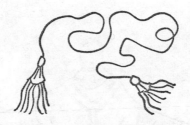

Cincture: A braided cord of linen used as a belt around the alb. It symbolizes the chastity required of the priest.

Maniple: No longer used by the Roman Catholic Church (but used in some Anglican parishes), this ornamental vestment made of silk or damask was worn over the left forearm. In ancient times, men wore a handkerchief this way to use to wipe the sweat from eyes and brow. The maniple symbolized the labor and hardship of the priestly ministry.

Stole: This is a wide band of fine cloth worn over the shoulders of a priest (or over the right shoulder and across the chest of a deacon). It is actually a narrow version of the Roman toga, which was worn wrapped around the body. In the Eastern Christian churches, the stole is wrapped in a particular way around the body. The stole is the chief symbol of priestly power, derived from Christ, and it is worn at the Eucharist and in administering all the sacraments.

Chasuble: This garment covers all the others and bears the symbolic colors of the feasts and liturgical seasons. It symbolizes charity, the love that makes our lives holy and graceful. There used to be a custom that the design of a cross be on both the front and back of the chasuble, to symbolize the "yoke of Christ," who said, "Take my yoke upon you, for my yoke is easy and my burden light." This is the yoke (a device for binding oxen or horses together to haul a load) of unselfish service that should be the mark of a priest.

Dalmatic: An outer garment with sleeves but colored like the chasuble, and worn by the deacon. It symbolizes joy in the life of dedicated service to God.

Hierarchical Insignia. These are the articles used by bishops, abbots and cardinals as signs of their offices.

Miter: The headgear worn by bishops and abbots. It has two points, one in front and one in back, and is worn in processions and other solemn occasions. Some have suggested that its form represents the Fish (ICHTHUS) that proclaims, "Jesus Christ, the Son of God, the Saviour" (see p. 96).

Ring: The circle is the symbol of eternity, and rings are worn by bishops as a symbol of their authority, which unites the Church of today with the apostles, and of their teaching, which unites us to the saving work of Christ.

Crosier: This staff of authority symbolizes the Good Shepherd, Jesus, whose presence should shine through the ministry of the bishop. Shepherds guide their sheep with a similar kind of crook, or crosier, prodding the slow ones with the straight end, and pulling back the fast ones with the curved end.

Pallium: This is a special strip of woolen cloth marked with crosses that is given by the Pope to the principal bishop of a particular part of the world. It is the symbol of an archbishop.

Cardinal's red hat: This wide-brimmed hat was given by the Pope to those who were to be considered special advisers to the Pope. These cardinals would also become the body who

would elect the next Pope. Today, all cardinals must be bishops, but this was not always the rule. Also, a smaller hat is now given to new cardinals. However, if you ever visit St. Patrick's Cathedral, in New York City, go behind the high altar and look far up into the vaulting overhead. There you will see the wide-brimmed hats of the former cardinal archbishops of New York, who are buried in the crypt beneath the altar.

Ecclesiastical Heraldry. Abbots and abbesses, bishops, cardinals and popes, according to tradition, adopt a "coat of arms" upon installation or ordination to their positions of leadership in the Church. Of course, their insignia are not really a coat of arms, since that would be appropriate only to the European nobility, who bore arms (weapons) in the Middle Ages. Instead, the heraldry of church leaders reflects their town of origin, their family name, or the particular virtue or gift for which they are most grateful to God. Our present Pope is especially devoted to the Blessed Virgin Mary, so he has a large M set on a shield with the cross inscribed upon it. Pope Paul VI was named Giovanni Battista Montini, so his emblem included a "little mountain," which is *montino* in Italian. Pope John XXIII chose as his motto: "That they might know thee," a quote from the Scriptures (Jn 17).

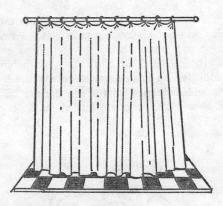

Sacred Textiles. Linen, silk, "purple stuff." Revelation 19:8: "Fine linen is the righteous deeds of the saints." Exodus 26–28: description of fine textiles used in the Tent of Meeting and the Ark of the Covenant.

Weaving has always reminded people of the long, patient labor of making things. It is not hard to compare weaving a great carpet, embroidered with flowers, fruits, trees, borders, birds, castles and clouds, to the work of God in the Garden of Paradise, the work of creation. Linen was used in the elaborate priestly robes of Aaron and his sons in the Book of Exodus and for the hangings and woven furnishings of the movable dwelling place of the Lord. Linen comes from the fibers in the stem of the flax plant, a gift of the earth. It is made into a sacred material by the careful labor of crafts persons, skillfully woven. It is thus fitting to use linen in vestments and cloths for worship, such as the corporal and purificator at Mass. Linen is also used in cinctures, albs, amices and fine chasubles. Linen is strong and durable and holds its shape during use, which makes vestments continue to appear full and beautiful.

Purple stuff was made from fine linen or silk cloth dyed with the pigment (a deep red) from the shellfish murex, which lives in the waters offshore from Lebanon. It takes many murexes to dye a small amount of cloth, so this fabric was expensive and used only by kings and in places of worship.

Scapular. Along with the hooded cowl, this is a symbol of monastic life. The scapular is worn as a hood with two wide strips of cloth in front and behind. When monastic communities began to have lay associates (oblates and tertiaries), the monks gave a small version of the scapular to the lay members to wear under their secular clothing.

The most common and popular scapular worn by lay people is the brown Carmelite scapular, which consists of two

small squares of stiff brown cloth held together with two lengths of brown string and worn around the neck. It is associated with devotion to Our Lady of Mount Carmel and the saints of the Carmelite Order. Other scapulars are signs of devotion to the Sacred Heart of Jesus and the Immaculate Heart of Mary.

The Body, Postures. "God created man in the image of himself" (Gn 1:26–27). Many great minds have tried to explain how this can be, but for our purposes, it is enough to know that we can show our love of God with the position and movement of our bodies as well as with words—thought or spoken.

Kneeling, we express our humility as creatures of God, close to the earth, yet rising upward from the ground. With straight backs, we focus our attention on meditation and offer ourselves completely to the will of our heavenly Father.

Prostrate, a position used in the ordination of a priest, we symbolize our complete willingness to be as clay in the hands of God. Just as Adam, the first man, was shaped from the ground (Gn 2), so in prostration we return to the ground to allow God to re-create us, to make new persons of us, to do new works in building God's Kingdom.

Standing, we proclaim our faith in the Resurrection of Christ, who did not remain prostrate in the tomb but rose again in the power of God. This is the posture we use whenever the gospel is read, when the Our Father is prayed at Mass, and when we receive Communion. See: Orante, illustration p. 35.

Movement: In more and more churches, sacred dance or movement is being used to express prayerful celebration. Processions are a form of sacred movement. At a solemn Eucharist, the priest incenses the altar by moving around the table, swinging the censer rhythmically and making the sign of the cross. The kiss of peace is another form of sacred movement at Mass. Have you ever participated in other forms of sacred dance?

Positions of the Hands.

Folded, or palms together. This symbol of prayer is experienced as the closing of a sacred circle formed by hands, arms and body. It is a gesture of concentration and embrace, especially fitting for devotional prayer in private.

Open hands. Palms cupped upward, hands and arms extended, we pray that our heavenly Father will give us the good things that we need, "our daily bread," both physical and spiritual. It is a gesture of complete trust and openness. See: Orante, illustration p. 35.

Holding the Eucharistic Host. With our left hand cupped beneath our right, we enthrone Christ, present in the Host, and we proclaim his Resurrection by holding the Host reverently with thumb and forefinger of the right hand. We respond to the priest's words "The Body of Christ" with the sacred sound of affirmation "Amen."

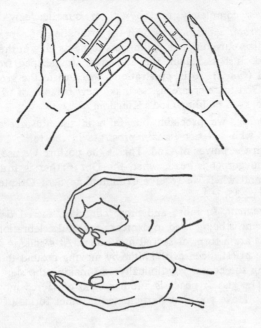

The sign of the cross. We begin each day and end each day with this gesture, which is the simplest way to affirm our Christian faith and willingness to follow Christ in the way of the cross and Resurrection. We bless our meals with this holy sign; parents bless their children with this holy movement. With our right hand we trace the cross from our forehead to our heart and to our shoulders left to right, showing that our bodies are temples of the Holy Spirit and that we have found life in the sign of Christ's victory.

FEASTS

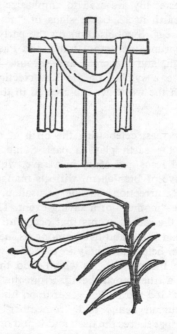

Easter. The heart of the Christian faith is the Paschal Mystery, that is, the passage of Jesus from death on the cross, to Resurrection on the third day. The day of the Resurrection is based on calculations of the movements of the sun and the moon. The spring equinox, when the day and night are of almost equal length in the northern hemisphere, falls on about

March 21. Easter Sunday is calculated to be the Sunday immediately after the first full moon after the spring equinox. The signs of sun and moon are used partly from the heritage of the Jewish computation of the date of Passover and partly out of reverence for the earth's own part in the Resurrection event. The earth itself is a symbol of Easter, because just after the spring equinox, living things begin to become more active, and the green plants sprout their new growth, following the apparent death of winter. Symbols of the Resurrection such as the Easter lily are used to emphasize this sign of renewal in the earth itself. Other signs of "new life" are the rabbit and the egg. Symbols used by the early Christians included the labarum, the empty tomb, the Paschal candle of the Easter Vigil, and the cross and shroud. The eight-sided baptistry is also a symbol of the Resurrection, "the eighth day," on which the world was re-created in the power of the Risen Christ.

Christmas. The feast celebrating the birth of Christ is also a day in which the earth plays a part. Some early paintings show the Child Jesus and Mary in a cave, which is meant to connect the cave of Bethlehem, with its manger, to the cave-tomb of the Resurrection, outside Jerusalem. In both cases, the earth is the "mother" of a saving event. The earth is thus made holy by the sacred events that occur on it. When Jesus became a human being and lived among us, he made all of us who are human beings also holy in a special way. This is the mystery of his Incarnation, by which God the Word is forever united to a true human being. From that time into eternity, whenever God the Father gazes upon his Son, he will always see a human being, and "remember" with love the human family that shares the flesh and blood of Jesus.

In addition to the manger and the images of Jesus in the arms of his blessed mother, Mary, European cultures have contributed a number of symbols to the celebration of Christmas. The mistletoe, a small plant that grows on the branches of the oak tree, was called "all-heal" by the ancient Druid priests of pre-Christian Europe. When the northern European

nations became Christian, they saw that the true Healer of all is Jesus Christ, and so used the mistletoe as a symbol of the Saviour. The holly has thorns and a blood-red berry, yet it is green even in the coldest part of winter. It symbolizes in advance the sufferings and death of Christ, and it hints of his victory over death and sin. The clinging ivy reminds us by its weakness (it must be held up by a tree or a stone wall) that we in our human weakness must cling to Christ for strength. Laurel, or bay, leaves have long been a symbol of victory. Conquerors wore laurel wreaths on their heads. So the evergreen laurel is also a symbol of the victory of Christ. All evergreen plants, especially pine and spruce trees, symbolize eternity and life everlasting, and so we deck our homes with their boughs at Christmas. Have you ever seen a builder put an evergreen bough at the high point of a roof? It is a symbol that the builder is relying on God's strength to preserve him and his workers from harm as they build. The poinsettia is a semitropical plant that blooms with great red bracts (leaves that take on color and act as petals do in some flowers) at Christmastime. The red is a color symbol of love for Christ, and the star-shaped bracts remind us of the Star of Bethlehem.

HOLY SOUNDS

Kyrie Eleison

Kyrie Eleison. The holy sounds of Christian worship have been set to music hundreds of times. They will no doubt continue to inspire musicians as long as the liturgy is celebrated. The musical sounds of prayer remain with us long after the celebration; they continue to be a source of prayerfulness at work and in quiet moments. The music continues to pray within us.

Kyrie eleison is from the liturgy of the Mass. It means "Lord, have mercy," in Greek (remember that the word *Kyrie, Kyrios,* was used to translate Yahweh from Hebrew into Greek). When we say, "Lord, have mercy," we are not pleading for mercy from an angry destroyer. We are praising God for his great mercy, shown in Jesus Christ. Kyrie eleison is the Church's word of praise and thanksgiving to our loving Father.

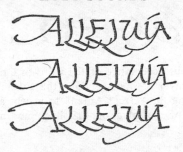

Alleluia. This is a Hebrew word meaning "Praise the Lord" (. . . *ia* is the short form, Yah, of Yahweh; *allelu* means "praise"). It is the great song of Easter joy. As St. Augustine said, "We are an Easter people and Alleluia is our song." During Lent, this song is silenced, but throughout the rest of the year the sung word Alleluia is a reminder that every day is a Paschal day, every day is a day of Resurrection for the followers of Christ.

Hosanna. This is a Hebrew word, addressed to Yahweh, meaning "Save, we ask." When Jesus entered Jerusalem (Palm Sunday, Mt 21:9, 15; Mk 11:9; Jn 12:13), the crowds recognized him as Messiah and Son of David with this word of hope and praise. We use it in the hymn "Holy, Holy, Holy, Lord God of Power and might . . . Hosanna in the highest," where it is a song of praise for the salvation that God has already brought about for us in Jesus.

Amen. A Hebrew word meaning "truly," "it is true." Jesus himself is named "the Amen" in Rv 3:14, because he is the one who is faithful to his word. We say, "Amen," to express

Amen

our faith and our acceptance of the word of God. At the end of the great prayer of thanksgiving (the Eucharistic Prayer) at Mass, we sing the "Great Amen" to accept and to express our gratitude for the salvation that has come to us in Jesus.

Maranatha

Maranatha. See 1 Cor 16:22 and Rv 22:20. An Aramaic phrase (Aramaic was the language that Jesus actually spoke) meaning "Come, our Lord," that is, "Come, Lord Jesus," as it was prayed in the Christian community of the earliest days. This phrase is a direct link for us between the hopes of Christians today and the hopes and prayers of the disciples of Jesus. As we say at Mass: "When we eat this bread and drink this cup, we proclaim your death, Lord Jesus, until you come in glory." This song of remembrance at the Eucharist reminds us that our communion is an act of thanksgiving for what God has already done for us and also a looking forward to the future that God is preparing for us.

VIRTUES

Virtue means power, energy, ability. To be virtuous is to be dynamic in the ways of goodness. It is also very much a matter of being a "gifted child" of God, from whom all good gifts come. The three "theological" virtues of Catholic tradition are *faith, hope* and *charity*. By faith, we mean complete trust in God, and confidence that God will lead us to himself according to a wisdom that is his alone. He has chosen each one of us and wants to work with us in the building of his Kingdom. The virtue of hope fills us with eagerness to cooperate in the work of the Kingdom. Hope also anchors us in the future, where the Lord waits for us with open arms. Charity, or love, is that full, selfless, giving love that we experience in God's embrace and that the Holy Spirit guides us in sharing with others. These three virtues are gifts that depend on the life and example of Jesus for their power and clarity. There are four other virtues that all persons strive for when they search for the good human life: justice, prudence, temperance and fortitude. The theological virtues complete and perfect these "cardinal" virtues by the action of the Holy Spirit. For example, if we consider how hope perfects the four cardinal virtues, we see that hope encourages us to strive for *justice* and fairness in our relations with others. Hoping for a spiritual future, we are made *prudent* in the important decisions of life. Hope also makes us practice *temperance,* or moderation, simplicity, and good taste in our use of the good things of life such as food, clothing, decoration and entertainment. Hope requires us to practice *fortitude* in the face of temptation and violence, because we look forward to a better life built on God's gift of love.

Hope is symbolized by an anchor. The anchor tells us that hope is a very strong force in the life of a Christian. Hope sets down firmly when the ship is in harbor and should not drift away; hope also shows us when we must move on, when the anchor has to be pulled up and the ship of the Church is being blown along by the wind of the Spirit of God to new ports and new discoveries.

VICES

The seven vices leading to the seven deadly sins are *pride, covetousness, lust, envy, sloth* (laziness), *greed* (gluttony) and *anger*. Habitually thinking or acting according to these tendencies leads us to a warped and wretched kind of living. Instead of coming to the fullness of life, as God intends, we sink into a subhuman state in which we cannot help others, and indeed, we find ourselves habitually hurting others. Sometimes these vices can be seen in individuals, and so they are represented by artists as "personification," that is, by drawing a person who has been warped and twisted by habitual sin. You can use your imagination to come up with some possibilities. We are also aware that whole nations can be addicted to certain vices, however. For example, if a nation uses up so much of the world's resources that millions of people in other countries are starving to death, that greedy nation is as gluttonous as any drunkard, and perhaps more so, since a weak person may have an excuse, but a wise and successful nation has no excuse except selfishness.

Our brother Jesus has come into our world to heal us of these seven vices by his example, his teaching, and his death and Resurrection. It is time to listen to him (Mt 5; 25).

BEASTS

Cock. The cock, or rooster, is well known in America as the weather vane, which, perched on top of barns and steeples, tells us the direction of the wind. The cock also reminds us of St. Peter, who repented of his three denials of our Saviour when he heard the cock crow. The wind is a symbol of the Spirit. The weather-vane cock tells us to repent, that is, to turn from sin and go in the direction of the Holy Spirit, and to walk with Christ, who is "the way, the truth, and the life."

Deer. (Jn 4:13, 7:37–38; Ps 42:1–2) The deer grows very thirsty as she runs through the forest, so she searches out the cool running brooks to quench her thirst. She knows where all of them are, and she is eager to be beside them. So, too, those people who love God long to be with him, and know where they can meet him at any time, any day of the year. The source of all the brooks of God's refreshing presence is the side of Christ, from which the blood and water of the sacraments flow. But Christ, present in our hearts at all times, is also a never-failing stream of joy and peace; he is a place in our hearts worth seeking with the same enthusiasm that the deer seeks out the sweet fresh forest streams.

Dolphin. The dolphin is not really a fish. Like the whale, it is a mammal, and it is very intelligent. The dolphin even communicates with its fellow dolphins and sings merrily. When the dolphins see a ship, they love to dance and dive along its bows. The dolphin leaps from the water and then dives deep into the sea, coming up again after a while for air, or else, just dives and leaps many times in succession. The dolphin's dancing at sea reminds Christians of Baptism, the deep plunge into the waters that bathe us into new life, and that remind us of the death and Resurrection of Jesus. The little leaps and dives remind us of the little joys and sorrows of everyday life, and even these are shared by Jesus, who is with us in all things.

Donkey/Colt. These are the beasts that bore Jesus into Jerusalem on Palm Sunday. They represent the humble character of Jesus' kingship, Son of David and Lion of Judah, but also suffering servant, man of sorrows, our brother as well as Lord. Jesus, though he was God, came among us as a man; manhood was the vehicle for his Godhead's journey among us. The donkey or colt represents his manhood, the humble means by which God comes among his people with hidden power to show his love and faithfulness.

Fish (ICHTHUS). The fish is totally immersed in the sea; since the coming of Christ, all the human race is immersed in God's freely given grace. Everywhere, the work of Christ is present to change people's lives. The Greek word for fish is

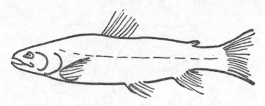

ICHTHUS. This is formed from the Greek letters representing the sounds of I, Ch, Th, U, and S, which are the first letters of each word in the Greek phrase translated as "Jesus Christ, the Son of God, the Saviour." You may have seen this mysterious acronym on bumper stickers.

When Jesus fed the five thousand, he multiplied both fishes and loaves. The fish always symbolizes the presence of the Saviour. The presence of the Saviour is inseparable from the Bread of the Eucharist.

Fox. Jesus called King Herod "that fox." This animal is associated in the bestiaries (medieval books describing the real and imaginary traits of real and imaginary animals) with stealth, sneakiness, shrewdness, cunning and "dirty tricks." The fox is quick to find ways to outwit the hunting dogs that pursue him. Hence, since dogs symbolize fidelity ("Fido"), the fox represents unfaithfulness, and skill in concealing one's lies.

Griffin. This strange, imaginary beast has all that we have said about other two-sided symbols. In one and the same symbol we find two powers, two forces. The eagle and the lion are joined in the griffin, symbolizing the two natures of Christ, true God and true Man. The griffin also reminds us that things are not always what they seem; good can be hidden in ugliness, and beauty can conceal evil. And the griffin is like us humans, combining the lion of pride and the serpent of disobedience. Or the body and the soul. Can you imagine other two-in-one combinations?

Jonah and the Great Fish (or "Whale"). This symbol of the Resurrection of Jesus is based on Jonah 1:16 and Matthew 12:40. To the ancient Israelites, nomads in the desert and farmers in the Promised Land, the great sea was a terrifying place in which great storms could occur almost without warning. If that were not enough, seafaring men told tales of great monsters that lurked in the deep, waiting to swallow sailors who fell overboard. People used to dry land were terrified of a bone-chilling death at sea, so the sea and its monsters came to symbolize the unknown terrors of death. Jonah, who was thrown overboard by the sailors and swallowed by a great fish, did not die; instead, God had the fish vomit him out on shore, because God had work for Jonah to do. He had to preach to the people of Nineveh and call them to repentance.

Jesus himself used this story to foretell his own suffering, death and resurrection; like Jonah, he would spend three days and three nights in the "belly" of the earth, as Jonah had done in the "whale." And like Jonah, he would come forth from the "jaws of death" to complete the task God had given him to accomplish.

Lamb. "Behold the Lamb of God," proclaimed John the Baptist when he saw Jesus. This Jesus is the Lamb that is to be slain for the sins of all persons, but the Lamb is a Passover Lamb, a Lamb whose death is for feasting, on the way to the great day of liberation. In ancient Jerusalem, the blood of animals was used as a symbol of purification and dedication to God. On the Day of Atonement (Yom Kippur), the Jewish High Priest sprinkled blood in the holiest part of the Temple, making peace between God and His people. The blood of Jesus on the cross also atoned; it made peace once and for all between God and humans.

The lamb is meek and gentle; its wool is white, pure, and useful in making warm clothes. The lamb submits to a quick death. It gives its blood so that others may live. It allows itself to be slaughtered; it is cooked and becomes a festive meal. So, too, Jesus is slain for us and, in the Eucharist, becomes a festive meal, a foretaste of the heavenly banquet in the Kingdom of God.

Lion. A symbol of royalty. The king of the family of David is called the Lion of Judah. The heroic presence of the lion suggests the power of a king.

Also, the lion is a symbol of pride, of roaring and displaying power by a human being in violation of God's supreme power. The human in rebellion against God's absolute authority over creation is doomed from the start; his roaring seems pathetic in comparison to the power of Christ's perfect obedience.

Ox and Ass. These are the two beasts that, according to legend, warmed the Child Jesus in the manger at Bethlehem. According to the prophet Isaiah (1:3), the dumb beasts are able to recognize, even in their simplicity, the presence of their Lord and Saviour, but King Herod and so many other humans do not.

Peacock, Pheasant. On the ancient mosaics of Rome, you may one day see the forms of wondrous birds preening, strutting, and bounding about, their long tails fanned out or long and winding. Why are these proud creatures adorning the walls of shrines? The pheasant, peacock and phoenix were all thought to be related as symbols of immortality and resurrection. The great tail of the peacock, with its many eyes, may still be seen in the half-circle windows of churches as a reminder of the glory of Jesus rising from the dead. Peacocks were so closely identified with the gods that ancient legends tell of their flesh being immune from decay. So, too, Christ did not remain in the tomb long enough to decay. Instead, he rose on the third day as a new creation that extends into our lives today.

Pelican. The pelican was thought to feed its young with blood from its own breast. In the medieval bestiaries, the pelican is often shown wounding itself with its sharp bill and caring for the chicks. Commentators observed that the pelican is like Christ, "by whose wounds we are healed" and who nourishes us with the sacrament of his Body and Blood.

Phoenix. An ancient legend tells of a fabulous bird of Arabia that lives five hundred years; then it burns itself to ashes.

After three days, a young phoenix rises from the ashes to begin a new life cycle. This story reminded the early Christians of the death and Resurrection of Christ, the Paschal Mystery, so the phoenix is often depicted in Christian art and fantasy.

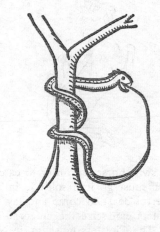

Serpent. The serpent is called wise and cunning, especially since the serpent was the tempter in Paradise who led Adam and Eve astray. But we also know that snakes are beautiful; their scales are formed in colorful patterns of light and dark bands. They move with great power and beauty without legs. As a symbol of evil, they warn us that sin and illusion may appear beautiful at first, but only later do we learn the sorrowful consequences of sin. Also, by their beauty, snakes can remind us that God can take sin and ugliness and reshape a life into something healed, forgiven and uniquely lovely. The snake is thus one of those symbols, like the door and the griffin, that point in two ways, toward both good and evil, darkness and light, hope and failure. The choice in life is not the snake's—it is *ours!*

Unicorn. This mythic creature has one sharp horn in the middle of its forehead. Its body is pure white, and like the strong

body of a stag or swift horse. In order to catch a unicorn, a pure virgin maiden must go into solitude in the woods and wait for this powerful beast to come and lay its head in her lap. Then the hunters can seize the unicorn. The great Unicorn Tapestries at The Cloisters museum, in New York City, depict this legendary hunt. The capture of the mighty unicorn requires the cooperation of a humble, chaste maiden, just as the coming of Jesus Christ required the assent of Mary.

PLACES

Hell. The Mouth of Hell. The illusion of sin is that we are entering a city of order, good sense, practical ability and pleasure. On the road to this city, we ignore the truth, which is that sin is a degradation of our human nature. The "mouth of hell" shows us in symbolic form, in the form of a door or portal in the earth, that sin is nothing more than gaping jaws, devouring our God-given human beauty to feed the ugliness of evil.

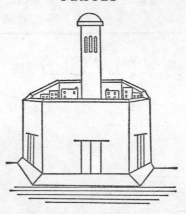

The Heavenly City. There are many symbols of the life we are promised in the presence of God after death. The Garden of Paradise, the stars in their movements (heaven means "sky") and the heavenly city are just a few. Above all, heaven is the place where we are all to be gathered in the sight of God as one lasting family, sharing the gifts of God as at a banquet, and feasting on enduring love.

Heaven. The Ladder of Jacob. The patriarch Jacob (also known as Israel) was a man of visions in which he experienced the presence of God. In one of his visionary dreams, he saw a great ladder ascending from earth to the heavens and angels ascending and descending on the ladder (Gn 28:10–15; Jn 1:51). Jesus himself used this vision to speak

of the coming of the Kingdom of God on earth in his own
Person. It is not enough to speak of "heaven up there." The
message of Jesus is that *God is with us,* now, in this life. If
our attitude is open, we, too, can see the Ladder of Jacob in
everyday living. This ladder is humility, and we ascend the
ladder of humility as we welcome life from day to day as full
of the gifts of God, leading us on to our eternal home.

Heaven. Cross and Crown. "If any would follow me . . . let
him take up his cross daily. . . ." The willingness to follow
Jesus daily, even if this means suffering and loneliness, is a
basic Christian attitude. The heaven side of this attitude is the
"crown," the reward of the vision of God, the experience of
his enduring love that erases all suffering and transforms

loneliness into communion. This is the mystery of heaven.
Another aspect of the cross and crown is that we must struggle here on earth to bring about the just and peaceful world
that God wills to establish as the crown of creation.

Jerusalem. Zion. Jerusalem, in some places referred to as the
City of Peace, will always be a symbol of the harmony and
wholeness of heaven. The earthly Jerusalem, with all its history of wars and divisions and sins, is still a place of pilgrimage today, because it reminds us that there is more to life than
power, money and pleasure. There are spiritual values for
which we strive, guided by the fiery winds of the Holy Spirit.
Living the virtues in close, prayerful union with Christ,

searching for God amid the symbols and events of this world, is the great human and Christian adventure. It is the adventure that takes us to Golgotha, where Christ was crucified, and it takes us to the empty tomb of the Resurrection. It takes us to the Mount of Olives, where Jesus ascended to the Father, there to prepare a lasting celebration for all of us at the end of time, when signs and symbols will fade and the Reality, the Eternal Banquet of Christ, will be shared by all who have hoped and hungered for so long.

The holy Mount Zion, in Jerusalem, is called the "mother of all the nations" (Ps 87), because on this mount, where the Temple stood, we are all spiritually born. Zion is the center of the spiritual world, where we are all children of God and where God comes to meet us. We are all secretly drawn to that one meeting ground with the One God, where all nations will dance and sing together the praises of the Lord. Zion is a symbol of the Church, where all nations are welcome to serve the Lord, as their heart and center, in peace. This peace is based on the reality that all human beings are brothers and sisters, taught by Jesus to call God "Father," and to ask for the Kingdom of the Father, the heavenly Jerusalem, to come into our world, even now, as we await the fullness of life.

INDEX